How to Write a Novel Using the Zettelkasten Method
Ana Mafalda Damião

How to write a novel using the Zettelkasten Method

How to write..., Volume 1

Ana Mafalda Damião

Published by Ana Mafalda Damião, 2024.

While every precaution has been taken in the preparation of this book, the publisher assumes no responsibility for errors or omissions, or for damages resulting from the use of the information contained herein.

HOW TO WRITE A NOVEL USING THE ZETTELKASTEN METHOD

First edition. August 20, 2024.

Copyright © 2024 Ana Mafalda Damião.

ISBN: 979-8227784629

Written by Ana Mafalda Damião.

Also by Ana Mafalda Damião

Autoconocimiento y Desarrollo Espiritual
Ángeles en nuestra vida: cómo contactarlos y vivir en sintonía con el universo
El poder de Saint Germain
Símbolos e imágenes para predecir el futuro
Rituales para la conexión - Diosas Celtas

Aventuras para crianças
Paco: Uma Aventura de Coração

Como escrever...
Como Escrever um Romance com o Método Zettelkasten

Cómo escribir...
Cómo escribir una novela con el Método Zettelkasten

Desenvolvimento Pessoal e Espiritual

Meditação Kind/mindfulness: Programa de 84 dias para mudar a sua vida

How to write...
How to write a novel using the Zettelkasten Method

Self-awareness
Therapeutic Writing - the Power of Writing in Personal Transformation

Self-Knowledge and Spiritual Development
Angels in Our Life - How to Contact Them and Live in Harmony with the Universe
Symbols and images to predict the future

Standalone
Escrita Terapêutica - o poder da escrita na transformação pessoal
Escrever...o quê? 20 + 8 ideias criativas
Escribir... 20 + 8 Ideas Creativas
Anjos na nossa vida - como contactá-los e viver em sintonia com o universo
Oráculo Das Bruxas
Símbolos E Imagens Para Prever O Futuro
Cristalomancia - A Arte Da Adivinhação Com Cristais
Dominomancia - A Arte Da Adivinhação Com O Dominó
Petit Lenormand - Como Interpretar
O Poder de Saint Germain

Rituais de conexão - Deusas celtas
Connection Rituals – Celtic Goddesses
The Power of Saint Germain
Ten Plagues of Egypt
Little Lenormand - How to interpret
Petit Lenormand - Cómo interpretar

Watch for more at https://www.instagram.com/therapeuticbooks/.

Table of Contents

1. Introduction

1.1 Presentation of the Work

Welcome to the Guide on the Zettelkasten Method for Novel Writers!

This book was created to help novelists organize their ideas and create more cohesive and structured stories using the Zettelkasten method.

The Zettelkasten method, which means "slip box" or "note box" in German, is a knowledge organization technique that allows for efficient creation and connection of notes, facilitating the development of a complex and well-planned novel.

Here, you will find detailed explanations, practical examples, and step-by-step guidance on how to apply this methodology to your writing.

1.2 What is the Zettelkasten Method

Origin and Definition

The Zettelkasten method was developed by the German sociologist Niklas Luhmann, who used this technique to write over 70 books and hundreds of scientific articles. It is a system of interconnected notes that allows for the effective storage, organization, and retrieval of information.

Main Components

- Atomic Notes: Each note should contain a single idea or concept.
- Links and Connections: Notes are linked to each other through cross-references, creating a network of knowledge.
- Index: An indexing system to facilitate navigation and location of the notes.

1.3 Why Use the Zettelkasten Method to Write a Novel

Benefits of Organization

- Facilitates the organization of complex ideas and plot details.
- Allows for structured development of characters and storylines.
- Helps maintain consistency and cohesion throughout the narrative.

Stimulating Creativity

- By connecting different notes, new ideas and relationships emerge, enriching the novel's plot.
- The method encourages the exploration of different angles and perspectives, increasing the story's depth.

Efficiency in the Writing Process

- Reduces the time spent searching for information and references.
- Improves efficiency in the revision and editing phases, as all information is organized and accessible.

1.4 Structure of the Book

Chapters and Sections

- This book is divided into chapters that cover everything from preparation for writing to the completion of the novel.
- Each chapter contains detailed sections with practical guidance and examples.

Practical Use of Zettelkasten

- The approach is practical, with examples of notes, connections, and how to apply the method at different stages of writing a novel.

Additional Resources

- At the end, you will find additional resources, such as examples of recommended tools, complementary readings, and note templates to start your own Zettelkasten.

1.5 How to Use This Book

Sequential or Selective Reading

- You can read the book sequentially to understand the entire process or skip to specific sections as needed.

Gradual Implementation

- Don't worry about implementing everything at once. Start slowly, applying the techniques as you feel comfortable.

Interaction and Feedback

- Use this book as an interactive guide. Take notes, experiment with the suggestions, and adjust the method to suit your preferences.

Writing a novel is a challenging journey, but with the right tools, it can be a rewarding and enriching experience.

I hope this book helps make your creative journey more organized and productive.

Ready to Begin?

Let's dive into the world of the Zettelkasten method and discover how it can transform the way you write your novel!

2. Understanding the Zettelkasten Method

2.1 Origin and History of the Zettelkasten Method

Niklas Luhmann and the Development of the Method

Niklas Luhmann was a German sociologist who created the Zettelkasten method during the 1960s. He used this system to manage his ideas and references, resulting in extraordinary productivity: over 70 books and hundreds of academic articles throughout his career.

Luhmann's Zettelkasten consisted of thousands of small paper slips (zettels) organized in boxes. Each slip contained a single idea or concept, with cross-references to other related slips.

Evolution of the Method

With the advancement of technology, the Zettelkasten method began to include digital tools, allowing for even more efficient organization and retrieval of information. Software like Roam Research, Obsidian, and Zettlr are popular among modern adherents of this method.

2.2 Basic Principles of the Zettelkasten Method

Atomic Notes

Notes should be atomic, meaning each note should contain only a single idea or concept. This facilitates the combination and connection of ideas.

Example: Instead of writing a long note about a character, create separate notes for each aspect of the character, such as appearance, backstory, motivations, etc.

Links and Connections

The strength of the Zettelkasten lies in the connections between notes. Use links to connect related notes, creating a network of knowledge that facilitates navigation and the discovery of new ideas.

Example: A note about the protagonist can be linked to notes about key plot events, other characters, and themes explored in the novel.

Index and Organization

A good indexing system is crucial. This can be a traditional index, a tagging system, or a combination of both. The goal is to make it easier to locate specific notes.

Example: Use tags to categorize notes by type (character, plot, setting) or theme (love, revenge, redemption).

2.3 Recommended Tools for Zettelkasten

Physical Notebooks

Although less common nowadays, some writers still prefer physical notebooks. Use paper slips or notebooks with dividers to organize your notes.

Keep an index at the beginning of the notebook and use numbers or codes to connect related notes.

Software and Applications

- **Roam Research:** Excellent for creating a network of interconnected notes. It allows for automatic backlinks and easy navigation between notes.
- **Obsidian:** Offers an intuitive interface and the ability to visualize the network of notes as a graph.
- **Zettlr:** A free and open-source markdown editor specifically designed for the Zettelkasten method.

Other Useful Tools

- **Notion:** Versatile and customizable, it can be adapted to function as a digital Zettelkasten.

- **Evernote:** Popular for note-taking, although not specifically designed for Zettelkasten, it can be used with some adaptations.

Practical Examples

Creating Atomic Notes

Imagine you are developing a character named "Alice." Instead of creating a single long note, create several smaller notes:

- Alice's Appearance
- Alice's Backstory
- Alice's Motivations
- Alice's Relationships with Other Characters

Establishing Links and Connections

Connect the note about "Alice's Motivations" with plot events that influence those motivations. For example, if Alice lost a loved one, create a note about that event and link it to her motivations.

Tips for Implementation

Consistency is Key

Maintain the habit of creating atomic notes and establishing links regularly. Consistency will make it easier to navigate and use your Zettelkasten.

Regular Review

Periodically review your notes and connections. This will help reinforce existing connections and discover new relationships between ideas.

Adaptability

Adapt the method to your needs. The Zettelkasten is flexible and can be modified as your writing process evolves.

3. Preparation for Writing

Before you start writing your novel using the Zettelkasten method, it's crucial to undertake meticulous preparation. This section of the book covers the essential steps to begin the creation process, from defining the theme and genre of your novel to the initial setup of your Zettelkasten system.

3.1 Defining the Theme and Genre of the Novel

To begin, it's fundamental to have a clear understanding of the central theme and genre of your novel. This will serve as the backbone of your narrative and guide all subsequent stages of the process.

Consider:

- **Identifying the Theme:** Determine the central message or idea you want to explore in your novel. It could be love, courage, revenge, redemption, among other themes.

- **Choosing the Genre:** Decide which genre your novel best fits into. Historical romance, science fiction, fantasy, contemporary romance, for example.

Having these elements clear from the start will help you focus your research and create notes more effectively.

3.2 Initial Research: Gathering Information and Inspirations

Once the theme and genre are defined, the next step is to conduct initial research, that is, gather relevant information that will fuel the development of your story.

Some activities include:

- **Reading and Studying:** Research books, articles, and other sources that can provide insights into the chosen theme and genre.
- **Visual Inspiration:** Explore images, videos, and artworks related to your theme for visual inspiration and setting.
- **Interviews or Personal Experiences:** If necessary, interview experts or draw from your own experiences related to the theme of the novel.

The research phase is crucial to ensure that your notes and ideas are grounded in a solid base of knowledge and inspiration.

3.3 Creating Your Zettelkasten: Setting Up the System

With the theme defined and the initial research completed, it's time to set up your Zettelkasten system.

• • • •

Essential Steps:

- **Choosing the Tool:** Decide whether you prefer a physical Zettelkasten (using index cards or notebooks) or a digital one (using software like Roam Research, Obsidian, Zettlr, Notion, among others).
- **Initial Structuring:** Establish basic categories for your notes, such as characters, plots, themes, settings, etc. This will help with the organization and retrieval of information during the writing process.
- **Indexing and Tags:** Implement an efficient indexing system. Use tags to categorize notes according to themes, characters, or any other category relevant to your story.

- **First Notes:** Start creating your first notes. Remember to keep the notes atomic, meaning each note should contain a single idea or concept. This will make it easier to connect the notes in the future.

4. Collecting and Organizing Notes

Collecting and organizing notes effectively is crucial for the success of the Zettelkasten method in writing a novel. A well-defined structure and the use of principles such as atomic notes and cross-references ensure that you have a solid foundation of information to develop characters, plots, and scenes in a cohesive and consistent manner.

4.1 Types of Notes: Ideas, Characters, Plots, Scenes, Research

Before you start writing, it's important to identify the different types of information you will need to organize.

Here are some examples of types of notes that can be created:

- **Central Ideas:** Notes that capture key concepts, main themes, or messages you want to explore in your novel.
- **Characters:** Create individual notes for each main and secondary character, detailing their backstory, physical characteristics, personality, motivations, etc.
- **Plots and Storylines:** Develop notes that describe the main plot, subplots, key events, and turning points in the story.
- **Scenes:** Note down ideas for specific scenes you plan to include in the novel, such as important dialogues, descriptions of settings, and evoked emotions.
- **Research:** Keep notes with detailed information on historical, scientific, cultural, or geographical elements relevant to your narrative.

4.2 How to Write Effective Notes

To ensure your notes are useful and effective, here are some guidelines you can follow:

- **Clarity and Conciseness:** Keep your notes straightforward and concise. Each note should contain only one specific idea or concept.
- **Relevant Detailing:** Include details that are relevant to the development of the story or to the understanding of characters and plots.
- **Use of Examples:** When appropriate, use concrete examples to illustrate your points. This helps to make your notes more vivid and easier to understand.
- **Cross-Referencing:** Establish links and cross-references between related notes. This helps build a network of connections that enriches the understanding of your narrative universe.

4.3 Structure of a Zettelkasten Note

Although the structure of each note may vary depending on the content, it is helpful to follow a basic structure that facilitates the organization and retrieval of information:

- **Clear Title:** Choose a descriptive title that succinctly summarizes the content of the note.
- **Body of the Note:** Clearly and organizedly describe the main content of the note. Use paragraphs or bullet points to divide related information.
- **Tags and Categories:** Use tags or categories to classify the note in terms of theme, character, plot, etc. This makes it easier

to search and organize within your Zettelkasten system.

- **Links and References:** Include links to other related notes or external references that can enrich the content of the note.

5. Connecting the Notes

In this section of the book, we explore the importance of establishing meaningful connections between notes within your Zettelkasten system. This not only helps organize information but also promotes the discovery of new ideas and insights throughout the process of writing your novel.

5.1 The Importance of Connections Between Notes

The Zettelkasten method heavily relies on the idea that knowledge is more powerful when interconnected.

Key points about the importance of connections between notes:

- **Creation of a Knowledge Network:** By connecting related notes, you create a knowledge network that allows you to explore themes, characters, and plots in a more profound and interconnected manner.
- **Facilitates Navigation:** Connections make it easier to find relevant information when needed. You can follow links between notes to explore different aspects of a theme or character.
- **Stimulates Creativity:** New ideas naturally emerge when you find unexpected connections between seemingly distinct concepts. This enriches the complexity and originality of your narrative.

5.2 Creating Links and Cross-References

To maximize the potential of Zettelkasten, it is important to establish effective links between notes.

Some best practices:

- **Bi-Directional Links:** Whenever possible, create links that work both ways (backlinks). This means that each note not only points to other notes but is also referenced by them. Tools like Roam Research facilitate the automatic creation of backlinks.
- **Cross-References:** Besides direct links, use cross-references within the text of your notes. For example, when discussing an important event in the story, reference the notes of the characters involved or the subplots affected by that event.
- **Tags and Categories:** Use consistent tags or categories to group related notes by themes, characters, or any other relevant categorization. This helps to quickly find correlated information during writing and revision.

5.3 Using Tags and Categories

Categorization through Tags or Labels is a Powerful Technique for Organizing and Connecting Notes

Helpful tips:

- **Defining Tags:** Choose tags that are descriptive and relevant to the content of your notes. For example, you can have tags for different characters, main themes, important locations, etc.
- **Tag Hierarchy:** Consider a hierarchy of tags if you're dealing with a large volume of notes. This can help structure your Zettelkasten in a more organized and intuitive way.
- **Search by Tags:** Use the tag search functionality in your Zettelkasten tool to find all notes related to a specific tag. This is useful for thematic reviews or revisiting specific ideas during writing.

Effectively connecting notes within your Zettelkasten not only improves information organization but also stimulates creativity and facilitates the exploration of complex ideas. By establishing a robust network of connections between themes, characters, plots, and scenes, you create an environment conducive to developing a cohesive and engaging novel.

6. Developing the Plot

Developing the plot using the Zettelkasten method goes beyond merely outlining the story from beginning to end. It allows for an in-depth exploration of the events, characters, and themes that make up the narrative. By creating and connecting notes that represent different parts of the plot, writers can build a story rich in detail and complexity while maintaining the flexibility needed for adaptations and refinements as the writing process progresses.

6.1 Building the Narrative Through Notes

To develop the plot using the Zettelkasten method, it's essential to follow some fundamental steps:

- **Identification of Key Plot Elements:** Start by identifying the key events and turning points that will form the structure of your plot. Each of these events can be represented by individual notes detailing what happens, who is involved, and what the consequences are.
- **Chronological or Structural Organization:** Depending on the nature of your story, you can choose to organize the notes chronologically (if the story follows a linear timeline) or structurally (if there are multiple plotlines that intertwine or develop in parallel).
- **Use of Mind Maps or Flowcharts:** Visual tools like mind maps or flowcharts can be helpful for graphically visualizing the structure of the plot. These diagrams help to understand how different events are connected and contribute to the development of the narrative.

6.2 Using Zettelkasten to Structure the Plot

The Zettelkasten method offers specific advantages for structuring the plot of your novel:

- **Flexibility and Adaptability:** Since the notes are independent and interconnected, you can adjust the plot as new ideas emerge or as the story develops in unexpected ways.
- **Detailing Subplots:** In addition to the main plot, you can use notes to develop subplots and secondary stories. These notes can be interlinked with the main plot or with each other, creating a complex web of relationships within your Zettelkasten.
- **Continuous Review and Refinement:** As the plot evolves, you can review and refine the connections between notes. This helps ensure that all parts of the story are cohesively integrated and that there are no contradictions or gaps in the narrative.

6.3 Visual Tools: Mind Maps, Flowcharts

In addition to textual notes, consider using visual tools to assist in plot development:

- **Mind Maps:** Ideal for brainstorming and visualizing non-linear connections between ideas. Each node can represent an important plot event, character, or theme, and the links between nodes show the relationships between them.
- **Flowcharts:** Useful for representing the sequence of chronological or structural events in the story. They provide a clear view of the narrative progression and the interactions between plot elements.

7. Character Development

Developing characters using the Zettelkasten method goes beyond just creating detailed biographies; it involves deeply understanding who these characters are, what motivates them, and how they relate to the world around them. By connecting notes that represent different aspects of the characters, you can build complex psychological portraits that drive the narrative and provide a rich experience for the readers.

7.1 Creating Detailed Character Profiles

To develop characters using the Zettelkasten method, consider the following steps:

- **Identification of Essential Characteristics:** Create individual notes for each main character, detailing their physical appearance, personality, life story, distinctive traits, and any other relevant characteristics.
- **Motivations and Conflicts:** Explore the internal motivations of the characters, their goals, desires, and emotional conflicts. Create specific notes for each of these aspects, connecting them to the main character notes to understand how these elements influence their decisions and actions throughout the story.
- **Interpersonal Relationships:** Develop notes that detail the relationships between the characters. What are the emotional dynamics, conflicts, or alliances that exist between them? Use links and cross-references to connect the notes of different characters when their stories intertwine.

7.2 Connecting Characters with the Plot and Themes

Use Zettelkasten to explore how the characters relate to the main plot and themes of the novel:

- **Thematic Connections:** Create notes that discuss how a character's personality traits align with the central themes of the story. For example, how does a character's past influence their current choices, and how does this contribute to the development of the plot?
- **Character Arc:** Develop notes that outline each character's development arc throughout the story. How do they change or evolve based on the experiences they go through? Connect these notes to specific events in the plot to show the causes and effects of the characters' emotional or psychological transformations.
- **Exploration of Motivations:** Use Zettelkasten to deeply investigate the motivations behind the characters' actions. Connect notes that detail crucial events in a character's life with their current decisions, helping to build a narrative rich in subtext and meaning.

7.3 Exploring Character Motivations and Arcs

This is a crucial step in creating three-dimensional and captivating characters:

- **Deep Motivations:** Beyond superficial motivations, explore the deeper and unconscious motivations of the characters. This can be done by creating notes that investigate their family background, past traumas, unfulfilled dreams, or ingrained beliefs that shape their choices.
- **Evolution Over Time:** Use the Zettelkasten to track the evolution of characters over time within the story. Create notes

that represent key moments of transformation or self-discovery, connecting them with other notes to show the characters' continuous progress.

8. Writing the Novel

Writing a novel is a complex process that requires planning, creativity, and discipline. The Zettelkasten method offers a structured approach that not only facilitates the organization of ideas but also promotes the cohesion and consistency of the narrative. By applying this method during writing, you can not only improve the efficiency of your creative process but also ensure that the final product is a well-structured and captivating work.

8.1 Planning Chapters and Scenes

Before you start writing, it's important to plan the structure of the novel:

- **Organization by Chapters:** Create notes that represent each chapter of your novel. Describe what happens in each chapter, which characters are involved, and how it contributes to the development of the plot.
- **Sequencing Scenes:** Plan the sequence of scenes within each chapter. Connect notes that represent each scene, including information about the setting, present characters, main dialogues, and important events.
- **Narrative Consistency:** Maintain cohesion throughout the novel by connecting the notes of each chapter and scene. This helps ensure that all events are logically sequenced and that there are no contradictions in the timeline or characterizations.

8.2 Using Zettelkasten to Maintain Cohesion and Consistency

During the writing process, the Zettelkasten method can be a powerful tool for maintaining narrative consistency and integrity:

- **Quick Reference:** Use links and cross-references between notes to revisit important information while writing. This is useful for recalling character details, past events, and main themes that need to be sustained throughout the story.
- **Tracking Subplots:** Use subplot and secondary event notes to ensure that all stories within the novel are satisfactorily developed and have appropriate resolutions.
- **Adapting to Changes:** The Zettelkasten is flexible enough to allow adjustments during the writing process. If new ideas arise or if the story's direction changes, you can easily add new notes and adjust existing connections.

8.3 Revision and Editing: Refining the Text with the Help of Zettelkasten

After completing the first draft, the Zettelkasten method remains useful during the revision and editing stages:

- **Structural Analysis:** Use Zettelkasten to review the overall structure of the novel. Check if all plot elements are logically connected and if the narrative flows coherently.
- **Character Enhancement:** Revisit character notes to ensure that their evolution throughout the novel is consistent and convincing. Adjust character motivations and actions based on notes detailing their development arcs.
- **Identifying Gaps:** Identify any gaps in the story, inconsistencies in characterizations, or areas that need more development. Create new notes or adjust existing connections to resolve these issues.

9.1 Authors Who Used the Zettelkasten Method

Umberto Eco

Umberto Eco, the famous author of *The Name of the Rose,* was known for his meticulous and structured approach to writing. Eco used a method similar to Zettelkasten, where he kept detailed notes of his research, reflections, and ideas. He organized his notes in a card system, categorized by topics, which allowed him to quickly access relevant information during the writing process. By adapting the method to his needs, Eco was able to create complex and well-structured works with remarkable narrative depth.

Roland Barthes

Roland Barthes, a famous literary critic and theorist, also employed a system similar to Zettelkasten. He maintained a detailed archive of his observations and insights on various texts and theoretical concepts. This method of organization allowed Barthes to develop his ideas in a cohesive and articulate manner, resulting in influential works such as *Camera Lucida* and *Mythologies.* Zettelkasten helped Barthes establish connections between different topics and build a robust argumentation in his writings.

Niklas Luhmann

Niklas Luhmann, a German sociologist and the creator of the Zettelkasten method, also wrote fiction. He used his extensive note archive to develop complex characters and plots in his novels. Luhmann adapted Zettelkasten for literary writing, where each note or idea was interconnected, allowing him to explore different perspectives and deepen the psychology of his characters. His innovative method resulted in works rich in detail and with an intricate narrative structure.

9.2 Achieved Results

Clarity in Narrative Structure

Authors like Umberto Eco and Roland Barthes found greater clarity in narrative structure by using the Zettelkasten method. The ability to efficiently organize ideas and information allowed them to construct cohesive and well-structured narratives. Easy and quick access to specific notes helped in crafting complex plots without losing coherence.

Deep Character Development

Niklas Luhmann, by applying Zettelkasten to character creation, was able to develop deep and multifaceted psychological profiles. The interconnection of notes related to different aspects of characters allowed for richer and more intricate character development.

Characters: The interconnection of notes related to different aspects of characters allowed him to explore their motivations, internal conflicts, and evolutions throughout the plot. This method resulted in more realistic and engaging characters.

Efficiency in the Writing and Revision Process

All the mentioned authors benefited from the increased efficiency provided by the Zettelkasten. The systematic organization of notes reduced the time spent searching for information and allowed for a more continuous writing flow. Additionally, during revision, easy access to notes helped identify inconsistencies and refine the narrative with greater precision. These examples demonstrate how the Zettelkasten method can be adapted to meet the specific needs of writers, contributing to the creation of high-quality literary works.

9.3 Examples of Notes and How They Connect

To illustrate how notes can be created and organized using the Zettelkasten method, let's use a fictional example of a novel in development. Imagine we are writing a mystery novel.

Example 1:
Note: Main Character
Note Title: Detective John Smith
Content:

- Full Name: Johnathan Edward Smith
- Age: 45
- Occupation: Private Detective
- Personality: Meticulous, observant, cynical
- Background: Former police officer, left the force after a traumatic incident
- Motivation: Solve cases to find personal redemption

Note: Traumatic Incident
Note Title: John's Traumatic Incident
Content:

- Description of the Incident: During a police operation, John accidentally shot a colleague.
- Consequences: John left the police force, started drinking, and eventually became a private detective.
- Link: [[Detective John Smith]], [[Bank Robbery Case]]

Example 2:
Note: Main Location
Note Title: Bar "The Refuge"
Content:

- **Location:** City center
- **Description:** A rundown bar where John spends much of his time.
- **Owner:** Sam, a longtime friend of John.
- **Important Events:** Meeting with informant Clara about the

bank robbery case.
- **Tags:** #location #recurring

Note: Bank Robbery Case
Note Title: Bank Robbery Case
Content:

- **Date of the Robbery:** March 12, 2022
- **Crime Details:** Bank robbery with hostages, $2 million stolen
- **Suspects:** Group of ex-military
- **Informants:** Clara, provided crucial leads
- **Link:** [[Bar "The Refuge"]], [[Detective John Smith]]

Explanation of the Connections
Each of these notes is interconnected in a way that creates a network of information, facilitating the development of the novel.

- **Detective John Smith** is directly connected to the note about the **Traumatic Incident**, which details the event that changed the main character's life. This connection helps deepen the reader's understanding of John's motivation and behavior.
- The note about **Bar "The Refuge"** is connected to both the **Bank Robbery Case** and **Detective John Smith**. This shows that the bar is a recurring and important location in the plot, serving as a meeting point and the setting for various subplots.
- The **Bank Robbery Case** is connected to several other notes, including informants and locations, which helps build a rich and interconnected setting where the story's events unfold.

These connections not only facilitate the organization of ideas but also promote greater cohesion in the narrative, allowing the author to maintain continuity and develop characters, plots, and themes throughout the work.

Practical Simulations of Using the Method

Practical Exercises

To help you practice creating notes using the Zettelkasten method, we offer some simulations and exercises based on common situations in novel writing. These exercises will allow you to experiment and become familiar with the process of creating and interconnecting notes.

Exercise 1: Developing a New Character

Hypothetical Scenario: You are creating a new character for your novel. This character will be the main antagonist.

1. **Creating the Character Note**

   Note Title: Antagonist - Dr. Marcus Raven

   Content:
   - Full Name: Marcus Alistair Raven
   - Age: 52
   - Occupation: Renowned scientist, specializing in biotechnology
   - Personality: Cold, calculating, ambitious
   - Background: Grew up in an orphanage, always obsessed with overcoming his limitations and proving his worth
   - Motivation: Desire for power and control, believes he can "improve" humanity through his research

2. **Creating Related Notes**

   Note: Secret Project

   Content:
   - Project Name: Project Nexus
   - Objective: Develop a virus that can control human minds
   - Link: [[Antagonist - Dr. Marcus Raven]]

Note: Conflict with the Protagonist
Content:

- Protagonist: Detective John Smith
- Nature of the Conflict: John tries to stop Marcus from releasing the virus
- Link: [[Antagonist - Dr. Marcus Raven]], [[Detective John Smith]]

Exercise 2: Planning a Plot Twist
Hypothetical Scenario: You are planning a plot twist where the protagonist's trusted ally is revealed as a traitor.

1. **Creating the Plot Twist Note**
   Note Title: Plot Twist - Sam's Betrayal
   Content:
       - Character: Sam, owner of "The Refuge" bar
       - Plot Twist: Sam is secretly allied with Dr. Marcus Raven
       - Motivation: Sam was blackmailed by Marcus to help with his plan
       - Impact: John feels betrayed and loses trust in his allies
2. **Creating Related Notes**
   Note: Revelation Scene
   Content:
       - Location: Bar "The Refuge"
       - Description: John discovers the betrayal by finding evidence in Sam's office
       - Link: [[Plot Twist - Sam's Betrayal]], [[Bar "The Refuge"]]

Note: Consequences of the Betrayal
Content:

- John must now work alone
- Distrust in other allies
- Link: [[Plot Twist - Sam's Betrayal]], [[Detective John Smith]]

Exercise 3: Exploring a Specific Theme
Hypothetical Scenario: You want to explore the theme of redemption in your novel.

1. **Creating the Theme Note**
   Note Title: Theme – Redemption

Content:

- **Description:** The protagonist's journey seeking redemption for past mistakes
- **Related Characters:** Detective John Smith, Dr. Marcus Raven
- **Key Scenes:** Final confrontation where John saves innocents and faces Marcus

2. Creating Related Notes

- **Note:** Redemption Scene
  - **Content:**
    - **Location:** Marcus's Laboratory
    - **Description:** John deactivates the virus and rescues the hostages, finding his redemption
    - **Link:** [[Theme - Redemption]], [[Final Confrontation]]
- **Note:** Character Arc - John
  - **Content:**
    - **Evolution:** From a tormented ex-cop to a redeemed hero
    - **Crucial Events:** Traumatic incident, conflict with

Marcus, final act of heroism
- **Link:** [[Theme - Redemption]], [[Detective John Smith]]

Exercise 4: Creating Atomic Notes

Example: Maria, a historical romance author, starts her Zettelkasten by creating atomic notes for each historical fact she wants to include in her book. Each note contains a single piece of information, such as "The Battle of Hastings occurred in 1066" or "Queen Victoria was crowned in 1837."

Application:

- **Atomic Note:** "The Battle of Hastings occurred in 1066"
- **Connection:** This note can be connected to other notes about characters involved in the battle, weapons used, and the battle's impact on English history.

Character Development

Example: João, a science fiction author, uses the Zettelkasten method to develop his characters. He creates a note for each character with basic details, followed by additional notes for specific characteristics such as personality traits, skills, and background.

Application:

- **Atomic Note:** "Character: Captain Zork"
- **Detailed Note:** "Personality Traits: Brave, impulsive"
- **Detailed Note:** "Skills: Experienced pilot, strategist"
- **Connection:** Notes about Captain Zork can be connected to events in the story where he demonstrates these characteristics and skills, creating a rich network of information.

Plot Planning

Example: Sofia is writing a detective novel and uses the Zettelkasten method to plan her plot. She creates notes for each scene, describing the setting, the characters present, and what happens. Each scene is linked to other scenes to maintain story continuity.

Application:

- **Atomic Note:** "Scene 1: The Crime"
- **Details:**
    - **Location:** Abandoned mansion
    - **Characters:** Detective Silva, Victim: Mr. Thompson
    - **Event:** Detective Silva finds Mr. Thompson's body
- **Connection:** The note "Scene 1: The Crime" is connected to the note "Scene 2: Initial Investigation," where Detective Silva begins gathering clues.

Revision and Editing

Example: Carlos uses Zettelkasten to review and edit his manuscript. He creates notes with feedback from his beta readers and editors, each containing a specific improvement suggestion.

Application:

- **Atomic Note:** "Feedback: Chapter 3 - Better develop the villain's motivation"
- **Detail:**
    - **Suggestion:** Add a scene where the villain explains his motives in a monologue
    - **Connection:** This note can be directly connected to Chapter 3, making it easier to access and implement the feedback.

Fictitious Case Studies
Case Study 1: Historical Romance

- **Author:** Isabel

- **Project:** Novel about the French Revolution
- **Atomic Notes:**
  - "The French Revolution began in 1789"
  - "Character: Marie, a peasant woman"

Event: The Storming of the Bastille
Connections:

- The note "The French Revolution began in 1789" connects to the "Event: The Storming of the Bastille."
- The note "Character: Marie, a peasant woman" connects to the "Event: The Storming of the Bastille," where Marie participates in the uprising.

Case Study 2: Science Fiction
Author: Pedro
Project: Novel about a space mission
Atomic Notes:

- "Technology: Warp Drive Engines"
- "Character: Dr. Alex, chief scientist"
- "Event: First Interstellar Journey"

Connections:

- The note "Technology: Warp Drive Engines" connects to the "Event: First Interstellar Journey."
- The note "Character: Dr. Alex, chief scientist" connects to "Technology: Warp Drive Engines," where Dr. Alex is the creator of the technology.

Diagram and Images

Example: Marta, a fantasy author, uses diagrams and images to visualize the network of her notes. She creates a mind map that connects characters, locations, and key events.

Application:

- **Diagram:** A mind map with the center being "Main Plot," branching out into "Characters," "Locations," and "Events."
- **Image:** Illustrations of the main characters and the locations described in the book.

Connection: The diagram helps Marta maintain plot cohesion and remember the connections between different elements of her story.

9.5 Writing Challenges

Exercise 1:

Describing Settings

Objective: Practice creating atomic notes that detail specific settings in your novel.

Instructions:

- Choose an important setting in your novel.
- Create an atomic note describing the setting in one or two sentences. For example, "The medieval stone castle with tall towers and a drawbridge."
- Create additional notes for specific details of that setting, such as: "The throne room is decorated with tapestries and chandeliers."

  Activity:
- Complete a set of 10 atomic notes for different settings in your novel.

  Example Notes:
- Note 1: "The medieval stone castle with tall towers and a

drawbridge."
- Note 2: "The throne room is decorated with tapestries and chandeliers."

Developing Characters
Exercise 2: Character Traits
Objective: Detail specific character traits using atomic notes.
Instructions:

- Choose the main character of your novel.
- Create an atomic note with a general characteristic of the character. For example, "Maria is a fearless and curious young woman."
- Create additional notes for specific traits, such as "Maria has brown hair and green eyes" and "Maria is an archaeologist and speaks five languages."
  Activity:
- Complete a set of 10 atomic notes for a main character.
  Example Notes:
- Note 1: "Maria is a fearless and curious young woman."
- Note 2: "Maria has brown hair and green eyes."
- Note 3: "Maria is an archaeologist and speaks five languages."

Connecting Notes
Exercise 3: Building Connections
Objective: Practice creating connections between notes to develop an interconnected network of information.
Instructions:

- Choose three atomic notes created in the previous exercises.
- Identify possible connections between these notes. For example, "Maria explores the medieval castle in search of artifacts."

- Create connection notes detailing how the chosen notes relate to each other.
  Activity:
- Complete a set of 5 connections between different notes.

Example Connections:

- Note 1: "Maria is a fearless and curious young woman."
- Note 2: "The medieval stone castle with tall towers and a drawbridge."
- Connection Note: "Maria explores the medieval castle in search of artifacts."

Plot Planning
Exercise 4: Structuring Chapters
Objective: Use the Zettelkasten method to plan the plot of chapters in your novel.
Instructions:

- Choose a specific chapter of your novel.
- Create an atomic note for the main objective of the chapter. For example, "Chapter 1: Introduce Maria and her interest in archaeology."
- Create additional notes for important events in the chapter, such as: "Maria finds an ancient map" and "Maria decides to embark on an expedition."
  Activity:
- Complete a set of 5 atomic notes for events in a specific chapter.
  Example Notes:
- Note 1: "Chapter 1: Introduce Maria and her interest in archaeology."

- Note 2: "Maria finds an ancient map."
- Note 3: "Maria decides to embark on an expedition."

Review and Reflection
Exercise 5: Analyzing Connections
Objective: Review the connections created between the notes and reflect on their effectiveness in developing the plot.
Instructions:

- Review the connections made in the previous exercises.
- Evaluate whether the connections are logical and contribute to the development of the plot.
- Make adjustments or add new connections if necessary.
  Activity:
- Review and adjust a set of 10 connections between notes.
  Reflection Example:
- Revised connection: "Maria finds an ancient map in the medieval castle that leads her to start her expedition."

Writing Challenges Without Examples:
Challenge 1: Build a Chapter with Notes
Objective: Use atomic notes and connections to write a complete chapter.
Instructions:

- Select a set of atomic notes related to a specific chapter.
- Use the notes and connections as a guide to writing the chapter.
- Ensure that you include all the details and events mentioned in the notes.

Activity:

- Write a complete chapter using at least 15 notes.

Implementing Feedback
Challenge 2: Incorporating Suggestions
Objective: Practice incorporating feedback from readers and editors into atomic notes.
Instructions:

- Choose feedback received on a passage from your novel.
- Create an atomic note for the feedback.
- Create an additional note with a possible solution.

Activity:

- Complete a set of 5 notes with feedback and possible solutions.

10 Conclusion

10.1 Recapping the Benefits of the Zettelkasten Method

The Zettelkasten method offers a revolutionary approach to organizing and developing literary ideas, providing numerous benefits for novelists.

Structured Organization: Zettelkasten allows writers to organize their ideas in a clear and structured manner. With a system of interconnected notes, it becomes easier to track and develop complex concepts over time. This is particularly useful in novel writing, where the plot can become intricate and details numerous. The structure provided by Zettelkasten helps maintain the cohesion and consistency of the story, avoiding contradictions and facilitating the revision and expansion of ideas.

Character Development: Developing rich and authentic characters is essential for any novel. The Zettelkasten method aids in this process by allowing writers to systematically explore characters' motivations, development arcs, and relationships. By creating and connecting detailed notes on each character, writers can track their evolution throughout the story, ensuring that their actions and emotions are consistent and well-grounded.

Efficiency in the Writing Process: Zettelkasten increases efficiency at all stages of writing. From initial planning through development to final revision, the method facilitates the organization of ideas and the quick retrieval of relevant information. This reduces the time spent searching for notes and references, allowing writers to focus more on creativity and the quality of their writing.

11. Appendix

11.1 Glossary of Terms

Atomic Notes: Small units of information that represent a single idea or concept. In the context of Zettelkasten, each note should be self-explanatory and independent.

Links and Connections: Cross-references between notes that help build a knowledge network. Links are used to connect related concepts, making it easier to navigate between ideas.

Backlinks: Return links that indicate all the notes that refer to a specific note. This helps visualize how an idea is interconnected with others.

Indexing: A cataloging system that allows for the quick organization and location of notes within the Zettelkasten. This can be done through tags, categories, or reference numbers.

11.2 Tools for Writers

This chapter offers a comprehensive collection of resources that can assist writers at all stages of their creative process. By utilizing these tools, books, courses, and communities, you can complement the Zettelkasten method and enhance your writing, organization, and research skills.

Software Tools

- **Obsidian**
  - **Description:** Obsidian is a powerful note-taking and personal knowledge management application that uses markdown and efficiently interlinks notes.
  - **Features:**
    - Note interlinking
    - Customizable plugins

- ▪ User-friendly interface
  - ○ **Use in the Zettelkasten Method:** Ideal for creating and organizing atomic notes, facilitating the interconnection of ideas.
- **Roam Research**

Description: Roam Research is a note organization tool that allows the creation of an interconnected knowledge database.

Features:

- Automatic backlinking
- Knowledge graph structure
- Bi-directionality-based interface
  Use in the Zettelkasten Method: Excellent for visualizing and managing the connections between notes.

Scrivener

Description: Scrivener is a long-term writing tool used by writers of all kinds.

Features:

- Organization of chapters and scenes
- Planning boards
- Integration with research tools
  Use in the Zettelkasten Method: Can be used to organize large volumes of text and interlink parts of your manuscript.

Zettlr

Description: Zettlr is a free and open-source markdown editor designed for academics and researchers.

Features:

- Markdown support
- Export in multiple formats
- Reference management
  Use in the Zettelkasten Method: An efficient tool for creating and organizing atomic notes with an academic focus.

Recommended Books

A System for Writing - How an Unconventional Approach to Note-Making Can Help You Capture Ideas, Think Wildly, and Write Constantly - A Zettelkasten Primer by Bob Doto, 2024

Antinet Zettelkasten - A Knowledge System That Will Turn You Into a Prolific Reader, Researcher and Writer by Scott Scheper, 2022

Atomic Note-taking - The Ultimate Zettelkasten Guide by Martin Adams, 2023

Building a Second Brain - A Proven Method to Organize Your Digital Life and Unlock Your Creative Potential by Tiago Forte, 2022

Digital Zettelkasten - Principles, Methods, & Examples by David Kadavy, 2021

Duly Noted - Extend Your Mind through Connected Notes by Jorge Arango, 2024

Effective Notetaking - Improve Your Learning Skills by Finding the Best Way to Select What's Important, Organize for Better Understanding, and More by Fiona McPherson, 2007

How to Take Smart Notes - One Simple Technique to Boost Writing, Learning, and Thinking - for Students, Academics, and Nonfiction Book Writers by Sönke Ahrens, 2017

Personal Knowledge Graph - Connected Thinking to Boost Productivity, Creativity, and Discovery by Ivo Velitchkov and George Anadiotis, 2023

Zettelkasten and the Art of Knowledge Management - Combine Your Learnings & Meaningful Life Events into a Personal Knowledge Graph Using Obsidian by Binny V A, 2023

Online Courses

Coursera: Creative Writing Specialization

Description: A series of courses focused on creative writing techniques, including plotting, character development, and style.

Use in the Zettelkasten Method: Complements the Zettelkasten method with creative writing techniques.

MasterClass: Neil Gaiman Teaches the Art of Storytelling

Description: A course offered by renowned author Neil Gaiman, covering all aspects of storytelling.

Use in the Zettelkasten Method: Learn from a master storyteller how to effectively structure and tell stories.

Udemy: Writing With Confidence: Writing Beginner to Writing Pro

Description: A course covering writing fundamentals, advanced techniques, and how to gain confidence as a writer.

Use in the Zettelkasten Method: Offers practical tools that can be integrated with the Zettelkasten method to improve writing.

Writer Communities

NaNoWriMo (National Novel Writing Month)

Description: An annual event that challenges writers to compose a 50,000-word novel during the month of November.

Use in the Zettelkasten Method: Participate in the community and use the Zettelkasten method to plan and organize your novel.

Reddit: r/writing

Description: An active community of writers on Reddit where you can exchange tips, receive feedback, and participate in discussions.

Use in the Zettelkasten Method: Get feedback on your notes and connections, and learn from the experiences of other writers.

Scribophile

Description: An online platform for critique and collaboration where writers can share their work and receive detailed feedback.

Use in the Zettelkasten Method: Share your notes and manuscripts to receive feedback and continually improve.

11.3 Checklists

Practical Facilitators:

Checklists are useful for ensuring that the recommended steps are followed when implementing the Zettelkasten method.

Checklist: Character Development

- Character name defined.
- Physical appearance described.
- Personality detailed.
- Complete backstory.
- Clear motivations.
- Character arc outlined.
- Connections with other characters established.
- Additional notes complete.

Checklist: Plot Planning

- Main plot defined.
- Subplots identified.
- Clear starting point.
- Plot climax outlined.
- Final resolution planned.
- Connections between main events established.
- Additional notes complete.

11.4 Note Templates

Note templates are essential tools to ensure your notes are clear, concise, and well-organized. Here are some templates you can use:

Template 1: Basic Atomic Note

- **Note Title:**
- **Date:**
- **Content:**
- **Tags:**
- **Cross-References:**

Example:

- **Note Title:** Battle of Hastings
- **Date:** 07/14/2024
- **Content:** The Battle of Hastings occurred in 1066 and was a decisive event in the Norman conquest of England.
- **Tags:** history, battle, Hastings
- **Cross-References:** William the Conqueror; Norman Revolution

Template 2: Character Development

- **Character Name:**
- **Appearance:**
- **Personality:**
- **Backstory:**
- **Motivations:**
- **Character Arc:**
- **Connections with Other Characters:**
- **Additional Notes:**

Example:

- **Character Name:** Maria Silva
- **Appearance:** Brown hair, green eyes, medium height.
- **Personality:** Brave, curious, determined.
- **Backstory:** Maria is an archaeologist who has always dreamed of discovering ancient artifacts.
- **Motivations:** Desire to make a significant archaeological discovery.
- **Character Arc:** Maria starts as an inexperienced young woman and grows into a renowned archaeologist.
- **Connections with Other Characters:** Mentor: Dr. João Santos; Antagonist: Dr. Ricardo Almeida.
- **Additional Notes:** Maria has a fear of heights.

Template 3: Scene Planning

Scene Title: Chapter: Location: Characters Present: Scene Summary: Scene Objective: Conflicts: Outcome: Additional Notes:

Example:

- **Scene Title:** Meeting at the Castle
- **Chapter:** 3
- **Location:** Medieval Castle
- **Characters Present:** Maria, Dr. Ricardo Almeida
- **Scene Summary:** Maria meets Dr. Ricardo Almeida at the castle and discovers his true identity.
- **Scene Objective:** To reveal the antagonist.
- **Conflicts:** Maria is suspicious of Ricardo, leading to a verbal confrontation.

- **Outcome:** Maria decides to investigate Ricardo further.
- **Additional Notes:** Ricardo inadvertently reveals an important clue.

Theme Template

- **Central Idea:**
  - ○ **Description:** Define the central idea or main theme of the story. What do you wish to explore or convey through your narrative?
- **Examples:**
  - ○ **Description:** Provide specific examples of how the theme is manifested throughout the story. What scenes or events illustrate this theme?
- **Connections with Characters:**
  - ○ **Description:** Describe how the theme is related to the characters. How do their actions and development reflect the central theme?

12. FAQ about the Zettelkasten Method

Frequently Asked Questions

1. **What is the Zettelkasten Method?**
   The Zettelkasten Method is a personal knowledge management system that uses interconnected notes to help with the organization and development of ideas. It was popularized by sociologist Niklas Luhmann.

2. **How do I start using the Zettelkasten Method?**
   To begin, create short, independent notes for each important idea or piece of information you encounter. Ensure that each note has a unique identifier and link related notes together.

3. **What is the best tool to use for the Zettelkasten Method?**
   There is no universally "best" tool, but some popular options include Obsidian, Roam Research, and note-taking software like Notion. The most important thing is to choose a tool you feel comfortable using regularly.

4. **How should I structure my notes?**
   Each note should be concise and focused on a single idea or concept. Use clear titles, identify your notes with unique codes, and add links to related notes.

5. **How do I keep my Zettelkasten organized?**
   Regularly review your notes and update the links as new connections emerge. Organize notes into temporary categories if necessary, but avoid creating rigid structures that might limit the system's flexibility.

6. **What are common mistakes when using the Zettelkasten Method?**
   Common mistakes include creating notes that are too long, not regularly reviewing and updating notes, and not linking notes adequately. Another mistake is trying to follow the

method too rigidly without adapting it to personal needs.

7. **Can the Zettelkasten Method be used for all fields of study?**
   Yes, the method is flexible and can be adapted to virtually any field of study or work that involves knowledge management, from social sciences to arts and exact sciences.

Detailed Answers and Solutions

- **Problem:** I have too many notes and feel lost. How can I manage this?
  Solution: Regularly reevaluate your notes and prioritize linking related notes. Use effective search tools within your system to quickly find relevant information.
- **Problem:** My notes are too long and complex. What should I do?
  Solution: Break long notes into several smaller notes, each focused on a specific aspect of the information. This will make it easier to create links between them and make your Zettelkasten more efficient.
- **Problem:** I can't find connections between my notes.
  Solution: Invest time in reviewing and reflecting on your notes. Sometimes, connections may not be immediate but will emerge over time as new notes are added.

Don't miss out!

Visit the website below and you can sign up to receive emails whenever Ana Mafalda Damião publishes a new book. There's no charge and no obligation.

https://books2read.com/r/B-A-KSCEB-YPUSE

BOOKS2READ

Connecting independent readers to independent writers.

Did you love *How to write a novel using the Zettelkasten Method*? Then you should read *Angels in Our Life - How to Contact Them and Live in Harmony with the Universe*[1] by Ana Mafalda Damião!

[2]

Angels in Our Life, by Ana Mafalda Damião, the first book in the Self-Knowledge and Spiritual Development Collection, is a work that takes us on a journey to discover how we can live in harmony with angels and the universe. The author shares insights on the angelic hierarchy, the 72 Kabbalistic angels, and presents practical methods for contacting angels, using natural elements like flowers, crystals, essences, and candles. The author encourages readers to live a more harmonious life, recognizing the signs and angelic messages that surround us. She details the spiritual meaning and characteristics associated with each angel, helping readers to identify and strengthen their personal connection

---

1. https://books2read.com/u/mgYJKx

2. https://books2read.com/u/mgYJKx

with their guardian angel. Through visualizations, affirmations, and angelic meditations, she offers tools to integrate angelic wisdom and support into everyday life, promoting a more balanced existence aligned with the divine.

Read more at https://www.instagram.com/therapeuticbooks/.

Also by Ana Mafalda Damião

Autoconocimiento y Desarrollo Espiritual
Ángeles en nuestra vida: cómo contactarlos y vivir en sintonía con el universo
El poder de Saint Germain
Símbolos e imágenes para predecir el futuro
Rituales para la conexión - Diosas Celtas

Aventuras para crianças
Paco: Uma Aventura de Coração

Como escrever...
Como Escrever um Romance com o Método Zettelkasten

Cómo escribir...
Cómo escribir una novela con el Método Zettelkasten

Desenvolvimento Pessoal e Espiritual

Meditação Kind/mindfulness: Programa de 84 dias para mudar a sua vida

How to write...

How to write a novel using the Zettelkasten Method

Self-awareness

Therapeutic Writing - the Power of Writing in Personal Transformation

Self-Knowledge and Spiritual Development

Angels in Our Life - How to Contact Them and Live in Harmony with the Universe

Symbols and images to predict the future

Standalone

Escrita Terapêutica - o poder da escrita na transformação pessoal

Escrever...o quê? 20 + 8 ideias criativas

Escribir... 20 + 8 Ideas Creativas

Anjos na nossa vida - como contactá-los e viver em sintonia com o universo

Oráculo Das Bruxas

Símbolos E Imagens Para Prever O Futuro

Cristalomancia - A Arte Da Adivinhação Com Cristais

Dominomancia - A Arte Da Adivinhação Com O Dominó

Petit Lenormand - Como Interpretar

O Poder de Saint Germain

Rituais de conexão - Deusas celtas
Connection Rituals – Celtic Goddesses
The Power of Saint Germain
Ten Plagues of Egypt
Little Lenormand - How to interpret
Petit Lenormand - Cómo interpretar

Watch for more at https://www.instagram.com/therapeuticbooks/.